SCARY ADVENTURES AROUND THE WORLD

DO YOU DARE VISIT THE BIGFOOT TRAIL?

BY MEGAN QUICK

Enslow
PUBLISHING

Please visit our website, www.enslow.com. For a free color catalog of all our high-quality books, call toll free 1-800-398-2504 or fax 1-877-980-4454.

Library of Congress Cataloging-in-Publication Data
Names: Quick, Megan, author.
Title: Do you dare visit the Bigfoot Trail? / Megan Quick.
Description: Buffalo, New York : Enslow Publishing, [2024] | Series: Scary
   adventures around the world | Includes bibliographical references and
   index.
Identifiers: LCCN 2023003057 | ISBN 9781978536005 (library binding) | ISBN
   9781978535992 (paperback) | ISBN 9781978536012 (ebook)
Subjects: LCSH: Bigfoot Trail (Calif. and Or.)–Juvenile literature. |
   Sasquatch–Juvenile literature.
Classification: LCC F868.K55 Q53 2024 | DDC 917.94/21–dc23/eng/20230216
LC record available at https://lccn.loc.gov/2023003057

Published in 2024 by
Enslow Publishing
2544 Clinton Street
Buffalo, NY 14224

Portions of this work were originally authored by Therese Shea and published as *The Bigfoot Trail*.
All new material in this edition was authored by Megan Quick.

Designer: Tanya Dellaccio Keeney
Editor: Megan Quick

Photo credits: Series background Le Chernina/Shutterstock.com; cover, p. 1 randy andy/Shutterstock.com; p. 5 https://upload.wikimedia.org/wikipedia/commons/7/73/Russian_Lake_in_the_Russian_WIlderness.jpg; p. 6 NPS/Hannah Schwalbe/Flickr; p. 7 Rainer Lesniewski/Shutterstock.com; p. 9 (top) https://upload.wikimedia.org/wikipedia/commons/0/0e/Yolla-bolly-wilderness.jpg; p. 9 (bottom) Paul Brady Photography/Shutterstock.com; p. 11 Volodymyr Osypov/Shutterstock.com; p. 13 aleks1949/Shutterstock.com; p. 15 (top) Hills Outdoors/Shutterstock.com; p. 15 (bottom) https://upload.wikimedia.org/wikipedia/commons/d/de/Bigfoot_trap.jpg; p. 16 Tom Reichner/Shutterstock.com; p. 17 Tami Freed/Shutterstock.com; p. 19 https://upload.wikimedia.org/wikipedia/commons/0/03/US_199_Redwood_Highway.jpg; p. 21 Daniel Lane Nelson/Shutterstock.com.

Printed in the United States of America

CPSIA compliance information: Batch #CSENS24: For further information contact Enslow Publishing at 1-800-398-2504.

Find us on

CONTENTS

WHAT'S IN THE WOODS? 4

TRAIL BASICS 6

THE HIKE BEGINS 8

HEADING NORTH 10

MORE MOUNTAINS 12

BIGFOOT AND THE BUTTES 14

GETTING WILD 16

REACHING THE REDWOODS 18

DO YOU DARE? 20

GLOSSARY 22

FOR MORE INFORMATION 23

INDEX 24

Words in the glossary appear in **bold** type the first time they are used in the text.

WHAT'S IN THE WOODS?

A giant, hairy creature walks quietly through the woods. Suddenly it stops and lets out a loud, high scream! Is it a man? Is it an ape? Both? There are more questions than answers when it comes to Bigfoot.

No one has ever been able to prove that Bigfoot exists. But that has not stopped people from looking for the **mysterious** creature. Are you ready to go on a search for this man-ape? If so, you'll want to head to the Bigfoot Trail.

FIND THE FACTS

THE BIGFOOT TRAIL RUNS MAINLY THROUGH THE KLAMATH MOUNTAINS IN CALIFORNIA. THE AREA IS KNOWN FOR ITS MANY TREES AND PLANTS. THERE ARE 32 DIFFERENT KINDS OF CONIFERS (MOSTLY EVERGREEN TREES) ALONG THE BIGFOOT TRAIL.

Hikers on the Bigfoot Trail have a view of beautiful lakes, mountains, and trees.

TRAIL BASICS

Most Bigfoot sightings have happened in the part of North America called the Pacific Northwest. The Bigfoot Trail runs through this area. The hiking trail is mostly in California, with a small part in southwest Oregon.

The Bigfoot Trail is about 360 miles (580 km) long. Some areas are fairly wild and hard to hike. Most people choose to hike certain parts rather than the entire trail. The trail begins in the south at the Yolla Bolly–Middle Eel **Wilderness** and ends at the Redwood National Park to the north.

Bigfoot Trail
⇦ Panorama   .5Mi
⇨ Samuelson Rock   .6Mi

This map shows the trail's path through Northern California, with a short trip into Oregon.

OREGON

BIGFOOT TRAIL

NEVADA

CALIFORNIA

PACIFIC OCEAN

FIND THE FACTS

ECOLOGIST MICHAEL KAUFFMANN NAMED THE BIGFOOT TRAIL WHEN HE HIKED THE WHOLE TRAIL IN 2009. HE WAS MORE INTERESTED IN THE TREES AND PLANTS THAN SPOTTING BIGFOOT!

THE HIKE BEGINS

Your search for Bigfoot will cover a lot of area! The Bigfoot Trail includes rivers, mountains, and forests. The Yolla Bolly-Middle Eel Wilderness is named in part for the Eel River, which is found there. The river doesn't contain eels, but does have lamprey—fish that suck other fish's blood!

Most of this wilderness is located in the Mendocino National Forest. The highest point is Mount Linn, which rises 8,092 feet (2,466 m). This mountain is home to the rare, or uncommon, foxtail pine tree.

BIG FOOT XING

FIND THE FACTS

PEOPLE WHO SAY THEY HAVE "SPOTTED" BIGFOOT REPORT THAT THE CREATURE WALKS ON TWO FEET, STANDS BETWEEN 6 AND 18 FEET (2 AND 5.5 M) TALL, AND HAS A BAD SMELL.

HEADING NORTH

You'll need to rest up before leaving Yolla Bolly-Middle Eel Wilderness. It is a long hike north to the Trinity Alps Wilderness, an area with many mountains, **canyons**, and lakes. It has more than 600 miles (966 km) of trails and is popular with campers and hikers.

As you hike the Bigfoot Trail in the Trinity Alps, watch out for another large, hairy creature: the black bear! If you do see one, don't run. Speak in a loud voice and back away slowly with your arms raised.

FIND THE FACTS

BIGFOOT IS ALSO KNOWN AS SASQUATCH. THE NAME COMES FROM THE NORTH AMERICAN INDIAN WORD *SASQ'ETS*, WHICH MEANS "WILD MAN" OR "HAIRY MAN."

If you're able to climb Thompson Peak in the Trinity Alps, you'll enjoy this view of Wedding Cake and Mount Hilton.

MORE MOUNTAINS

Next stop on the Bigfoot Trail is the Marble Mountain Wilderness area. Here you will find more mountains and canyons as well as 89 lakes. Marble Mountain is an unusual **formation** of red and gray marble.

As you look around for any trace of Bigfoot, keep an eye out for bears, deer, and even wolverines, the largest members of the weasel family of animals. They have powerful jaws, sharp claws, and they can kill animals much larger than they are.

FIND THE FACTS

IN 1958, RAY WALLACE SAID HE FOUND GIANT FOOTPRINTS NEAR HIS WORKPLACE IN NORTHERN CALIFORNIA. THE STORY RAN ON THE NEWS AROUND THE COUNTRY. SOON BIGFOOT WAS FAMOUS.

Many reports of Bigfoot sightings describe a creature like the one seen in this illustration.

BIGFOOT AND THE BUTTES

As you continue north, you arrive at an area with two reddish-orange rock formations called Red Buttes (BYOOTS) Wilderness. Instead of sloping sides like a hill or mountain, a butte has very steep sides and a flat top. The buttes' color comes from the **metals** iron and magnesium in the rock.

There have been several Bigfoot sightings in the Red Buttes Wilderness area—one man even said he saw Bigfoot swinging on tree branches! Also in this area is the only Bigfoot trap in the world. It has only caught bears and is no longer in use.

The only known Bigfoot trap was built in 1974, after a miner found huge, human-like footprints in the area.

FIND THE FACTS

ABOUT 15 MILES (24 KM) OF THE TRAIL IN THE RED BUTTES WILDERNESS CROSSES OVER INTO OREGON. IT'S WORTH A VISIT TO CHECK OUT THE HUGE TREES: ONE DOUGLAS FIR MEASURES 31 FEET (9.4 M) AROUND THE TRUNK!

GETTING WILD

Your next stop is the Siskiyou Wilderness, which includes some of the most difficult hiking on the Bigfoot Trail. The Siskiyou Mountains cross the wilderness, making it tough for people to explore the area. (This could also make it an ideal place for Bigfoot to hide!)

While traveling through the Siskiyous, be on the lookout for rattlesnakes. These snakes are **venomous**, so watch out for their fangs. Some rattlesnakes in the wild have lost their noisy tail, so you may not hear the warning rattle.

Many trails in the Siskiyou Wilderness are hard to travel because of trees that have fallen across the paths.

FIND THE FACTS

THE SEARCH FOR ANIMALS THAT MAY OR MAY NOT EXIST, LIKE BIGFOOT, IS KNOWN AS CRYPTOZOOLOGY.

REACHING THE REDWOODS

You've made it! The final part of the Bigfoot Trail takes you on a walk through the Redwood National Park. Redwoods are the tallest trees in the world. They also live a long time! Some redwoods can live to be 2,000 years old.

You may see a figure creeping through the forest. Is it Bigfoot? No, it's a mountain lion! It's important to never hike alone in the park. These killer cats are more likely to attack a single hiker.

FIND THE FACTS

A REDWOOD NAMED HYPERION IS THE WORLD'S TALLEST TREE AT 379 FEET (115 M). PARK VISITORS AREN'T ALLOWED NEAR IT BECAUSE TOO MANY PEOPLE HAVE LEFT TRASH AND HARMED THE AREA AROUND THE TREE.

Bigfoot Trail ends among giant redwoods like these. Notice the size of the trees compared to the cars.

DO YOU DARE?

Rattlesnakes, bears, and mountain lions: do you dare hike the Bigfoot Trail for a chance to spot a creature that might not exist? Maybe not. But this **unique** trail offers much more than a possible Bigfoot sighting.

Many people are drawn to the area by the Bigfoot **legend**. They might not find the mysterious creature they are looking for. But as they search, their reward is the natural beauty of the mountains, forests, lakes, and rivers.

FIND THE FACTS

BIGFOOT IS NOW A TV STAR! THERE ARE MANY TELEVISION SHOWS ABOUT THE SEARCH FOR SASQUATCH: *EXPEDITION BIGFOOT*, *THE BIGFOOT PROJECT*, AND *SASQUATCH UNEARTHED*, TO NAME A FEW.

The views from the Bigfoot Trail are worth the trip even if you never spot the legendary creature.

GLOSSARY

canyon: A deep valley with steep sides.

conifer: One of mostly evergreen trees or shrubs that produce cones and have leaves like needles or scales.

ecologist: A scientist who studies the relationship between living things and their environment, or the place they live.

formation: A bed of rocks that make up one unit.

legend: A story that has been passed down for many years that is unlikely to be true.

metal: A hard, shiny element found in the ground.

mysterious: Difficult or impossible to understand.

unique: One of a kind.

venomous: Able to produce a liquid called venom that is harmful to other animals.

wilderness: A piece of land where no people live and is in its natural state.

FOR MORE INFORMATION

Books

Mayer, Amelia. *Hiking Activity Book for Kids: 35 Fun Projects for Your Next Outdoor Adventure.* Oakland, CA: Rockridge Press, 2022.

Ransom, Candice. *Legendary Bigfoot.* Minneapolis, MN: Lerner, 2020.

Websites

The Bigfoot Trail
www.bigfoottrail.org
Check out photos, maps, and cool facts about the trail.

Wonderopolis: Is There Any Proof That Bigfoot Is Real?
www.wonderopolis.org/wonder/is-there-any-proof-that-bigfoot-is-real
Explore the possibility of a real Bigfoot and then try some follow-up activities.

INDEX

bear, 10, 12, 14, 20

cryptozoology, 17

Eel River, 8

foxtail pine tree, 8

Kauffmann, Michael, 7

Klamath Mountains, 5

lamprey, 8

Marble Mountain Wilderness Area, 12

Mendocino National Forest, 8

mountain lion, 18, 20

Mount Linn, 8

Pacific Northwest, 6

rattlesnake, 16, 20

Red Buttes Wilderness, 14, 15

Redwood National Park, 6, 18, 19

Sasquatch, 10, 20

Siskiyou Wilderness, 16, 17

Thompson Peak, 11

Trinity Alps Wilderness, 10, 11

Wallace, Ray, 12

Yolla Bolly-Middle Eel Wilderness, 6, 8, 9, 10